Understanding
Islam™

History of Islam

Frances O'Connor

ROSEN
PUBLISHING®
New York

For Madeline, Anton, and Jack

Published in 2009 by The Rosen Publishing Group, Inc.
29 East 21st Street, New York, NY 10010

First Edition

Library of Congress Cataloging-in-Publication Data

O'Connor, Frances.
History of Islam / Frances O'Connor.
    p. cm.—(Understanding Islam)
Includes bibliographical references and index.
ISBN-13: 978-1-4358-5064-4 (library binding)
ISBN-13: 978-1-4358-5382-9 (pbk)
ISBN-13: 978-1-4358-5386-7 (6 pack)
1. Islam—History—Juvenile literature. 2. Islam—Juvenile literature.
I. Title.
BP50.O36 2009
297.09—dc22

    2008013556

Manufactured in the United States of America

On the cover: (*Top left*) Eighteenth-century gold calligraphy art work with the name of Allah and his prophet Muhammad. (*Bottom right*) Thousands of Muslims arrive at Mecca.

CONTENTS

Introduction

The story of Islam begins with a humble man who was devoted to practicing kindness toward others, and it continues with more than a billion followers in many countries. It is a story that begins with a prophet who preached the Oneness of God to his polytheistic society and insisted that people give their wealth to less fortunate people, a very unpopular idea in his time. Islam is an interesting, beautiful world religion that asks its followers to be mindful of God's commandments and the needs of others in their community.

In the aftermath of the terrible acts of terrorism on September 11, 2001, which shocked, saddened, and angered people the world over, many people in Western countries began to question the teachings of Islam. Sadly, it is often the case that violent political acts by militant Muslim groups obscure better understanding of Islam.

This illustration depicts Muhammad, the prophet of Islam, with his followers. Muhammad lived from 570–632 CE.

The History of Islam

Most Muslims are peaceful people who practice a religion that calls for personal responsibility and a commitment to upholding the rights of others, whether they share the faith of Islam or not. Islam teaches followers to love God and all humanity, and to root out injustice and oppression wherever it may occur.

THE ORIGINS OF ISLAM: MUHAMMAD AND HIS FOLLOWERS

Around the year 570 CE, a baby boy was born to a family in Mecca, a large trading city on the northwestern part of the Arabian Peninsula. Muhammad ibn Abd Allah was born into an Arab trading clan called Banu Hashim. Shortly before his birth, his father died. Muhammad's paternal grandfather, Abd al-Mutalib—one of the main leaders of Mecca—took the responsibility of caring for Muhammad and his mother. At birth, he was given to a foster mother, who nursed him, instead of his birth mother.

According to the local custom, Muhammad stayed with his foster mother's Bedouin tribe for a few years and then was returned to his mother. At age six, his mother took him to visit her brothers in Medina. On the way back home to Mecca, she suddenly fell ill and died. Sadly, when young Muhammad returned to Mecca, he met with more bad news—the death of his grandfather. After this death, he was taken in by one of his uncles, Abu Talib. Abu Talib was the head of the Hashim clan. He was

Muhammad meets the Christian monk Bahira. According to Muslim beliefs, Bahira immediately recognized that Muhammad was to be a prophet when he met the young man, who was traveling with his uncle in a trade caravan.

a very kind man but not very wealthy. In order to ease the financial burden on his uncle, the young Muhammad found work as a shepherd for a local family. As was usual for most people in his time, Muhammad didn't learn to read or write.

There isn't much information about the rest of Muhammad's growing-up years, but it seems that he probably worked as a camel trader. It is known that he accompanied his uncle in caravans to trade with other tribes on the Arabian Peninsula and in southern Syria, where he encountered the customs of other cultures. Later, he began working for a wealthy older widow named Khadijah. She grew to like Muhammad very much, for he was well known as being an honest, responsible person with whom to do business. Khadijah liked Muhammad so much that she proposed marriage. It's thought that he was around twenty-five years old at this time, and she was forty. When Muhammad married Khadijah, he became a respected member of the merchant class and was much admired by the Meccan elites.

Muhammad's Spirituality

Historical sources do not give much information about Muhammad's spirituality until he was around the age of thirty-five, but it is known that he never worshipped idols, which was unusual for a Meccan. At the time of Muhammad's birth, Mecca and the surrounding region, Hijaz, was the site of worship for three important idols, believed to be the "daughters of Allah," the One God. People came from western and central Arabia to worship at a sanctuary in Mecca called the Kaaba, the House of God. Arabians at this time believed that idols could communicate with the One God for them.

The Kaaba housed idols that represented not just the three goddesses but also other gods. Each year, it was a custom for local tribesmen to go on a hajj, or pilgrimage, to worship at the Kaaba and participate in ceremonial processions around the shrine. The Kaaba was built by their ancestor Abraham two thousand years before Muhammad's birth as a sacred place of monotheistic worship. In the years since, it had become more of a community gathering place, similar to a fair, and the worship of idols had overtaken the genuine worship of the One God. Muhammad was unusual for his time because he refused to worship the idols and tribal deities and instead sought to worship the One God of Abraham.

By the age of forty, Muhammad had begun to retreat for prayer in a small cave in the mountains near Mecca. Like his grandfather, Abd al-Mutalib, he spent the whole month of Ramadan in a cave in Jabal an-Nour, the "mountain of light." He prayed and meditated about the meaning of his life.

The First Revelation

According to Islamic belief, in approximately 610 CE, after about five years of annual retreat in the cave, the angel Gabriel appeared to Muhammad. Gabriel declared Muhammad a messenger of God and made him recite a set of sacred words coming from the Divine. Muhammad was scared at first and didn't believe his own eyes or ears. He thought he might be going crazy, so he ran from the cave back home to his wife, feeling shaken. However, Gabriel continued to appear to him every few days.

At first, Muhammad told only Khadijah the exact revelations he was receiving. Slowly, he shared these short yet powerful messages with a few close relatives and friends. As he gained courage, he started telling more people in his community. In 613 CE, Muhammad was commanded to go forth and publicly proclaim God's Oneness and denounce pagan deities that most Meccans continued to worship. He started preaching in the streets to call people to his religion, called Islam ("submission to God"). At first, he was ignored by most people. They figured he was preaching the same message that Christianity and Judaism taught—to believe in one powerful God, to be kind to others, and to know that the Day of Judgment was coming. Merchants who had traveled to other parts of the Arabian Peninsula had heard

In this illustration depicting one of the key incidents in the prophet Muhammad's biography, Muhammad receives his first revelation of God's word from the angel Gabriel.

similar words from the Christians and Jews that lived there, but the Arabs could not imagine giving up their tribal gods and changing their customs.

A problem soon emerged as new revelations received from the angel Gabriel required Muhammad to spread the message of helping others by bringing justice to slaves, giving money to the poor, and practicing acts of kindness toward everyone equally. Muhammad began to speak out more forcefully against the social injustices of Meccan society. Many of the common folk of Mecca accepted Muhammad's ideas and became Muslims, followers of

Islam. The wealthy traders and their powerful clans had been very happy with the existing state of affairs—namely, being rich, carefree, and in control.

The Meccan leaders were unhappy with Muhammad's call to abandon their deities in favor of the One God because they wanted to keep their ancestors' beliefs and maintain the status quo. As more Meccans became attracted to Muhammad's teachings, the Meccan elites felt it was necessary to stop Muhammad before he became too influential. The top Meccan clans turned against Muhammad and threatened him with violence. In order to remain safe, Muhammad realized that he and his followers had to leave Mecca. He had already sent some of his followers to refuge in the Christian land of Abyssinia to avoid Meccan prosecution. In 619 CE, the Muslims went to a city called Taif, not too far from Mecca, to seek asylum but were refused entry and had to return to Mecca.

The Move to Medina

The year 619 CE was a very sorrowful one in Muhammad's life for this and a few other reasons. Muhammad lost his most staunch supporter and confidant, his beautiful wife Khadijah, as well as his supportive and influential uncle, Abu Talib. Then, something amazing happened. One night, when Muhammad was asleep, he was awakened by the angel Gabriel. According to Muslim belief, Gabriel guided Muhammad on a journey to Jerusalem on a winged steed, and then from a rock there, Muhammad ascended to Heaven. During this experience, Muhammad met Jesus, Abraham, Moses, and other figures who are considered prophets. He then stood before God and was given glimpses of Heaven and Hell. Muslims believe that this journey signifies that Muhammad's message is a continuation of the message brought by the previous prophets of God.

After this trip, Muhammad felt encouraged to continue his mission. However, he still had to deal with the Meccans who were very unhappy with him. Meccan leaders were uncomfortable about the social changes taking place, and they began preparing to kill him, since he would not compromise his message. In 620 CE, Muhammad met a pilgrim in Mecca who explained that in

Muhammad is shown riding the horse Buraq during a miraculous journey from Mecca to Jerusalem in 619 CE known as the Isra and Mi'raj.

his home city of Yathrib, rival tribes were fighting bloody battles, and soon there would be chaos. The residents of Yathrib badly needed an arbitrator, someone to help them sort out their problems and bring peace. This pilgrim, having heard of Muhammad's reputation for being just and peaceful, invited him to Yathrib and pledged an oath of support and security to Muhammad.

Muhammad encouraged his followers to go north to Yathrib, where he would join them. In 622, Muhammad received word that a group of Meccans were planning to kill him. On the night of the assassination attempt, he

This manuscript illustration depicts Muhammad delivering a sermon in the Medina mosque after the Hijrah, or emigration from Mecca.

departed early with his close adviser Abu Bakr. They hid in a cave for three days, and according to the tradition, a spider made a web that covered the mouth of the cave just minutes before his pursuers searched the area. Muhammad and Abu Bakr then made their way to Yathrib, and this journey became known as the Hijrah, or migration. The event was so significant that it came to mark the beginning of the Islamic calendar and the beginning of the Muslim community as a political force in Arabia.

Conflicts in Medina and Mecca

There was a lot of work to do as the leader of a growing Muslim community. Muhammad had to welcome new Muslims as they came to Medina, teach Islam as he received the word of God, and help resolve the conflicts and quarrels between individuals and groups. He also made a series of agreements that helped bring his followers among the newly arrived Meccans and the local Medinans closer together. A document was written up stating that all groups' rights would be protected, including that of Jewish tribes in Medina, who were to be treated as members of the community so long as they adhered to the agreement of mutual support

LETTING THE CAMEL DECIDE

When Muhammad arrived in Yathrib, all of his followers were very excited to greet him, and each welcomed him to live with them. However, Muhammad's followers were comprised of two distinct groups: the newly arrived Meccan Muslims and the new converts native to Yathrib. Each group had its own culture and sense of pride, and each wanted the honor of receiving the Prophet. To avoid favoritism, Muhammad made a decision to let his camel roam free and make a home wherever it stopped. The camel guided him to an area where he then built several small brick rooms, one for each of the two wives whom he had married after the death of Khadijah. Muhammad and his followers also built the first mosque at this site, and, in honor of the Prophet's arrival, Yathrib was henceforth called Medina (short for Madinat an-Nabi, or "city of the Prophet").

and protection from the hostilities that were expected from the Meccan elites.

Until this time, while in Mecca, the early Muslims faced Jerusalem when making their daily prayers, since the Kaaba contained so many idols and Muslims were prevented from congregating at the Kaaba by the Meccan authorities. In Medina, tensions emerged between Muhammad and some Jewish tribes who were unsure about him and who enjoyed good, long-standing relations with the Meccans. According to Muslim belief, when Muhammad was repudiated by Jewish leaders who did not accept him as a true prophet, God instructed Muhammad to have his followers pray in the direction of Mecca. This was seen as a sign that Muhammad would have to deal with the Meccans sooner or later, and that part of his mission would be to restore the Kaaba's sanctity as the House of God.

The Muslim community in Medina faced many challenges. In particular, when the Meccan Muslims migrated there, they had no way to make money because they were not farmers like the Medinans, and most of their belongings left behind in Mecca had been confiscated by the Meccan tribes. Muhammad sent a party of his followers to raid the Meccan trade caravans that were coming through the area. This was a way for the followers to get supplies of food and other goods, as well as to demonstrate to the Meccans that the Muslims were not weak. The Arabs of this time were accustomed to this type of warfare and competition as a means of survival, and the Muslims felt justified in harming Meccan economic interests.

The Meccan elites, who were already opposed to Muhammad and his teachings, were very angry. In 624 CE, they sent a group of fighters with a large caravan, expecting Muhammad's followers to try to raid the goods. Sure enough, a small group of Muslims did try to take the animals, clothing, and food, and the two groups fought. Although the Muslims were severely outnumbered, they fought hard and won the battle. The Muslims took this as a sign of God's divine help and considered themselves chosen by God. The next year, in 625 CE, the Meccans came back to

An image depicting the Battle of Badr in 624 CE appears in a fourteenth-century manuscript, *Siyar-I Nabib* (Life of the Prophet), authored by a blind Turkish poet, Mustafa Darir, for Murad III, Sultan of Constantinople.

make up for the previous unexpected defeat. This time the Meccans won, killing and wounding many of the Muslims.

The following year, another great battle took place between Muhammad's followers and a huge number of Meccans. The Meccans tried to lay a siege of the city of Medina and made alliances with some of the Jewish tribes in the area. In preparation for the battle, Muhammad and his followers dug a trench in front of Medina so that the Meccans would be unable to get into the town, and the battle was over before it really began. The Muslims took the Meccans' inability to enter Medina as another sign that God was helping them. After this battle, wary of the Jewish tribes' relations with the Meccans, the Muslims drove out two of the three Jewish tribes of Medina. A third tribe of Jews, believed to have helped the Meccans plot against Muhammad, was dealt with more harshly. The men of the tribe were killed, and the women and children sold into slavery, a common outcome of war in pre-modern times.

After these three years of battles, the Meccans were starting to come to terms with Muhammad's growing power in Arabia, as more tribes accepted his message and allied with the Muslims. Muhammad and his followers set out from Medina to worship at the Kaaba in Mecca. When they got there, however, armed Meccans wouldn't allow them to perform any of the ritual ceremonies. Even though Muhammad insisted that he came in peace, they turned him and his followers away. The Meccans sent an emissary to create a truce with Muhammad to prevent further hostilities by either side, and Muhammad agreed to wait a year until he could return to Mecca to worship.

Conquering Arabia and Bestowing the Word of God

The next year, as promised, the Meccans allowed Muhammad and his followers to come to the Kaaba and perform their ceremonies peacefully. All looked to be peaceful between the Muslims and the Meccans. However, in the following year, pagan allies of the Meccans attacked a group of Muslims. When the news reached Medina, it was considered a breach of the agreement. Muhammad and about one hundred thousand followers

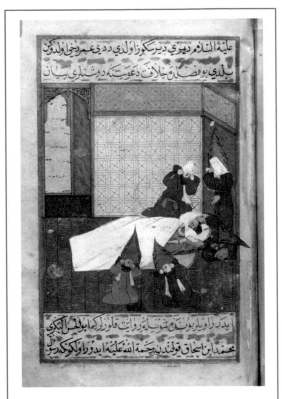

This manuscript image depicts Muhammad's death in Medina in 632 CE, soon after his final pilgrimage to Mecca.

marched into Mecca, where they were met by Abu Sufyan, the Meccan leader. He surrendered Mecca and the Kaaba to Muhammad rather than fight. Without any bloodshed or violence, Muhammad was able to win over Mecca. In a very important moment, Muhammad marched to the Kaaba, placed his hand on the black stone of the Kaaba, and declared, "Allahu Akbar," which means "God is the most Great." He then had his followers destroy the idols at the shrine, and it was never used again for worshipping any deity but the One God. The Kaaba remains the central site of worship for Muslims today.

Muhammad's stay in Mecca was short. Once he established control over Mecca, he returned to Medina. Arab tribes throughout the peninsula, having heard of Muhammad's success, became more inclined to accept his teachings and agreed to pay allegiance to him. After a short time, Muhammad controlled most of the peninsula, and new converts slowly adopted Islamic customs.

In 632 CE, Muhammad made his annual pilgrimage to the Kaaba, which would turn out to be his last. On the tenth day of his pilgrimage, Muhammad made his last great address to the Muslims. In his sermon, he stressed the equality of all people and the importance of upholding each other's rights. He told them to treat each other well and preserve the unity of Islam. At the end of his address, he noted that he had left the Book of God and his own life example (called *sunnah* in Arabic), which contained every-thing necessary to keep the believers free from error in their lives. Just after this, Muhammad left for Medina. At a stop along the way home, he acknowledged his younger cousin and son-in-law, Ali, as his heir and encouraged respect for him. Some weeks later in Medina, Muhammad became ill. He died on the twelfth day of Rabi I, the third month of the Islamic calendar.

Sunnis and Shiites

After Muhammad's death in 632 CE, there was a split in the Islamic faith that continues to this day. Muhammad died without naming the person who should become the caliph (successor), the next leader of the Muslims. The faithful at that time had differing ideas about who would lead and protect the community. Some Muslims thought someone in Muhammad's own bloodline should take his place, starting with his cousin and son-in-law, Ali ibn Abi Talib. Ali was married to Muhammad's daughter Fatimah. However, most Muslims believed the Prophet's successor should be elected from among his trusted companions.

Muhammad's friend and adviser Abu Bakr was chosen first to follow in Muhammad's footsteps. Abu Bakr died, and, after two other companions led for a number of years, Ali became the fourth caliph in 656 CE. Ali was murdered in 661 CE, near Kufa, which is a part of modern-day Iraq. Muslims continued to be divided as to whom should be caliph. Eventually,

Muhammad is shown here with his daughter Fatimah and her husband Ali. The flames surrounding Muhammad and Ali indicate that Ali is the rightful successor of Muhammad, being his cousin and son-in-law.

the dispute led to a formal split amongst the Muslims.

Most Muslims accepted the governor of Syria, Mu'awiyah, as the next caliph. They also accepted his son Yazid, marking the start of rule by a family dynasty known as the Umayyads. They didn't feel that the caliph needed to be related to Muhammad but simply a wise, strong person who would faithfully follow Muhammad's sunnah, or life's customs. This majority of Muslims would become known as Sunni Muslims. A minority of Muslims felt that only someone of Muhammad's bloodline could rightfully be the caliph. Those Muslims felt the next caliph should be Ali's son Hussein. They became known as Shi'at Ali, or partisans of Ali and his descendents. They are now known as the Shia or Shiite Muslims.

The Battle of Karbala

Hussein's supporters in Kufa invited him to come to them from Medina and promised to fight against Yazid on his behalf. On October 10, 680 CE, Yazid's forces encircled Hussein's entourage near Karbala, in modern-day Iraq. The surrounded group numbered less than one hundred and was

An Influential Minority

Today, the vast majority of Muslims are Sunni. Shiites account for only 150 to 200 million of the world's estimated 1.3 billion Muslims. That's less than 15 percent of the total population. Shiite Muslims make up the majority in the countries of Iraq, Iran, Bahrain, and Azerbaijan. They are minorities in Saudi Arabia, Egypt, Lebanon, and Pakistan but are still a significant presence. They outnumber Sunnis in the Middle East's major oil-producing regions. Outside Iran, Sunnis are the majority in most Muslim countries.

made up of Hussein's friends and relatives. All were killed in the course of several days, and Hussein's head was cut off. His body was left on the battlefield, and his head was taken to Yazid's court. The Umayyads had hoped this would end the Shiite movement, but instead it had the opposite effect. Hussein, in death, became a holy figure, or martyr. Hussein's followers believed he was brave to stand up against those whom they believed had taken his rightful role and who seemed to have abandoned the teachings of Islam. That belief continues to inspire and rally Shiite Muslims today. Their tragic deaths are mourned by all Muslims, but Ali and Hussein are specially revered figures in the Shiite faith.

A woman in Turkey observes Ashura, the day of mourning when Shiite Muslims remember the death of Hussein in his battle against Umayyad caliph Yazid. She is standing next to a painting of Imam Hussein.

Nearly 1,400 years later, Shiite Muslims continue to annually commemorate Hussein's death, during a time known as Ashura. It is a dramatic spectacle. They march in the streets and beat their chests. They cry in mourning. Some of the more devoted Shiites even hit themselves with swords and whips as a form of penitence for the injustices suffered by Hussein and his family at Karbala. For Shiite Muslims, the descendents of Muhammad were not merely caliphs (political rulers) but were imams as well, meaning they could provide religious guidance. This continued for almost two hundred years, until the mid-ninth century, at which point most Shiites believe the twelfth imam disappeared. His name was

Muhammad al-Mahdi, which means "the guided one." He disappeared at the location of what is now the Samarra shrine in modern-day Iraq. Most Shiites believe that he continues to live and is hidden from this world but will someday return, ushering in a period of justice before the end of time.

Survival Despite Oppression

The Muslims who accepted Umayyad rulers as political leaders did not consider them to have much religious authority as time went on. Religious scholars insisted that they were the only ones qualified to interpret the Qur'an and Muhammad's sunnah, although people should obey political authorities to ensure public order. To remain in good standing, the rulers usually accepted this division and tended to support this "Sunni" form of Islam. As a result, Shiite Muslims were sometimes persecuted and had limited opportunities to join the military or government.

Though many of their core religious beliefs were similar, the Shiites had some different faith practices, and Shiite scholars developed their own theological and legal positions based on their study of the Qur'an, the sunnah, and the teachings of the imams. Some Sunnis did not believe Shiites were true Muslims, just as Shiites saw Sunnis as deficient in their love for Muhammad's household. Historically, however, many Muslims have held a variety of beliefs incorporating Sunni and Shiite views. Extended families and tribes often contained members of both groups, and intermarriages between them have not been uncommon.

Still, the Shia doctrines of Islam continued to attract people in certain regions who were steadily converting to

This seventeenth-century mosque in Isfahan, Iran, was built in tribute to Sheikh Lotfollah Ameli, a Lebanese Shiite leader who was invited to Iran by the Safavidrulers. Verses from the Qur'an are written around the edges of its dome.

Islam as Muslim civilization continued to develop. Though there were fewer of them, Shiites spread throughout a large geographical area, often living next to or among the Sunni Muslims. No one region had a huge majority of Shiites until the sixteenth century, when the largely Sunni population of Persia (modern-day Iran) was required to convert to Shiism by the ruling Uh-zahr-I warriors who had come from what is now Turkey. Their leader, Shah Ismail, had adopted Shiism and felt his empire would be more unified if the inhabitants shared the faith. This marked an important development in Islamic history, since Shiite Muslims came to govern a large geographical area, Iran, that remains a predominantly Shiite country today.

The History of the Qur'an

The history of the holy book, the Qur'an, is a very important part of the Islamic religious time line. Muslims believe that this scripture, similar to what Jews believe of the Torah, has always existed with God in a "preserved tablet." They believe that once it was time for the Qur'an to be revealed to people through Muhammad, it was lowered into the lowest heavens on a special evening called the Night of Power (*Laylat al-Qadr* in Arabic). Some translations of the Arabic call this special night the Night of Predetermination, the Night of Destiny, or the Night of Almightiness.

The Qur'an itself says that this particular night was "better than a thousand months" because of the great meaning of what happened—God's words being delivered to Muhammad. The exact date of this night isn't universally agreed upon, though all Muslims believe that this night took place during the last third of the month of Ramadan. Sunnis typically celebrate it on the night of the twenty-seventh of Ramadan, while

Muhammad memorized the words of God given to him by the angel Gabriel and conveyed them to his followers, who memorized and wrote them down. The verses are known collectively as the Qur'an.

Shiites believe it took place on the nineteenth, twenty-first, or twenty-third of the month.

Listening to God

According to Islamic tradition, Muhammad received the Qur'an in a series of revelations through the angel Gabriel that lasted over a period of almost twenty-three years. From 610 to 632 CE, Gabriel appeared to him and revealed some of God's divine words and prayers. It's important to note that Muslims believe that Muhammad neither wrote nor edited the Qur'an. He didn't know how to read or write, which is why he was surprised when Gabriel commanded him to read the first time he appeared to Muhammad in the cave on Mount Hira. He answered Gabriel's command to read by saying that he didn't know how. When Gabriel commanded him again to read, Muhammad again insisted that he didn't know how. Muhammad finally agreed to recite what Gabriel presented to him. Over many years' time, Muhammad was to listen to these revelations, considered God's divine speech, and pray to God in the manner that Gabriel instructed.

The Writing of the Qur'an

After Muhammad's death in 632 CE, the verses that comprised the entire Qur'an were written down in a single manuscript, in a sequence previously specified by Muhammad during recitations. The caliph, Abu Bakr, was urged by another close companion, Umar ibn al-Khattab, to compile the Qur'an in written form after a battle at Yamama against hostile Arabian tribes, where many

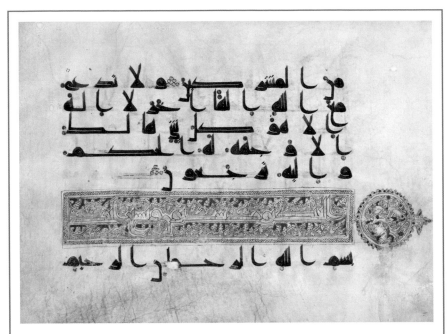

This early manuscript shows part of chapter 29 of the Qur'an. Zayd ibn Thabit, a scribe who knew the Qur'an by heart and was said to have been present when Muhammad recited the entire Qur'an back to the angel Gabriel before he died, was responsible for preserving the scripture in written form.

Muslims who were known to have memorized the Qur'an were killed.

Abu Bakr, in turn, asked Zayd ibn Thabit, the scribe of Muhammad, to collect the Qur'an because, according to tradition, Zayd was present when Muhammad recited the Qur'an to the angel Gabriel for the last time before he died. Zayd cross-checked with other Qur'an memorizers as he wrote out the verses that comprise the Qur'an in sequence, chapter by chapter. It has 114 chapters, called suras. Some chapters are very long, while some are short. The shortest chapter has only three verses, and the longest

These Muslim schoolgirls in Band Aceh, Indonesia, read, study, and memorize the Qur'an.

one has 287 verses. Once finished, Zayd gave Abu Bakr the first fully written copy of the Qur'an, which was put in the keeping of Muhammad's wife Hafsah. Muslims believe that the written text contains a precise record of the words that Muhammad received from Gabriel.

Since this early period, the text has remained unchanged, and all Muslims, despite differences in interpretation, consult the same scripture. The Qur'an was originally written in Arabic, but today there are many translations available for Muslims living all around the world.

How the Qur'an Is Taught

Traditionally, Muslims hear the Qur'an being recited from the moment of their birth. At an early age, Muslim youth are taught to memorize key parts of the Qur'an so they can recite them, and many children learn to read and write by copying verses of the holy scripture. Being able to recite the whole Qur'an is very highly valued in the Muslim community, and often believers will go to hear someone with a beautifully trained voice recite the verses.

Muslims study and memorize the Qur'an and hadith, which, when put together, form the main source material for Islamic law, called sharia. Sharia is thought of as "the way set out by God," rather than just law codes. In the early centuries of Islam, Muslim legal scholars gave shape to the sharia through reasoned interpretation of the scripture and hadith. This was done in order to provide a framework for religious practice, governance, economic life, social and family structures, and interreligious relations that would in their view represent the teachings and principles of Islam. Subsequent generations of Muslims have followed the interpretations of established schools of law. Since many conditions have changed in modern times, however, scholars today seek ways to offer fresh interpretations that they believe remain consistent with the teachings and principles of Islam.

Historically, the Qur'an has been taught in religious schools called madrassas. Students as young as nine and ten years old attend madrassas to learn to recite the whole Qur'an and learn the sunnah of Muhammad. In the past, this was the core of a much more comprehensive education, and religious scholars were among the most broadly knowledgeable people in society.

The true purpose of a madrassa is to be a place where young students first learn to read the Qur'an and then continue their religious studies in a well-balanced way. The madrassa, meaning "place of learning," has played an important role in Islamic history, and, as an institution, it was a precursor to the university in Europe.

The Qur'an, like other scriptures, continues to engage human beings seeking spiritual answers. It draws new followers to Islam every year, bringing new believers into the Muslim *ummah*, or community, each day. The Qur'an shapes the lives of Muslims today, just as it has done in the centuries since Muhammad first began preaching his message and performing acts reflecting the teachings of Islam.

The Spread of Islam Throughout the World

Islam has spread throughout the world in the last 1,500 years. While many Muslims live in the Middle East, there are many more outside the region, with significant populations in countries such as Indonesia, Pakistan, Nigeria, the Philippines, and the United States. To understand how Islam has spread across the globe, we must first look at its holiest sites: Mecca and Medina.

Mecca and Medina

Since Mecca is Muhammad's birthplace and the site of the Kaaba, it is one of the most sacred places in the world for all Muslims. It is located in modern-day Saudi Arabia, near the Red Sea coast. It has a population of just over one million people. Every Muslim is expected to travel to Mecca at least once in his or her lifetime if he or she is physically and financially able to do so. This important spiritual journey is called the hajj. Every year, millions of Muslims travel from all over the world to reach Mecca. People from all walks of life, various nationalities, and different races come together in Mecca to reenact

Masjid al-Haram is the Great Mosque in Mecca that surrounds the Kaaba. The current mosque's general plan dates to the fifteenth and sixteenth centuries, but it has been enlarged and equipped with the most modern technologies and materials.

important events associated with the prophet Abraham, who is considered an ancestor of Muhammad.

Modern-day Muslims still believe Medina is a sacred site because it became Muhammad's home. In Medina, Muhammad and his followers built a mosque. It was a simple and rough building. The roof was supported by tree trunks. A stone marked the direction in which the faithful should pray. When Muhammad preached, he stood on a tree trunk. It was from this humble spot that Islam spread throughout the world.

Islam Begins to Spread

Muhammad's followers formed an army to defend themselves against people who did not believe he was a prophet and who wanted him dead. For years, they battled with enemies within Medina and Mecca, as well as with tribes scattered around the area. They were great fighters and were often victorious. Muslims saw these victories as a sign from God that they had been chosen for a special purpose. When they lost a battle to the Meccans, the Muslims saw it as a test from God. Eventually, the Muslims were able to conquer the Meccans as well. As Muhammad's political strength grew, more Arabian tribes were willing to ally with him and accept his religious teachings. This was an important development for the growth of Islam. It increased the number of people following Muhammad. For some tribes, however, accepting Islam was a way to demonstrate political loyalty to Muhammad rather than a genuine expression of faith.

After Muhammad's death in 632 CE, some tribes that had converted to Islam broke away, considering themselves

Muslim pilgrims arrive for evening prayer at the Mosque of the prophet Muhammad in Medina, Saudi Arabia. Muhammad's tomb is enclosed inside the mosque, and Muslims visit Medina to pay their respects to him.

no longer answerable to the Muslims in Medina. Abu Bakr, who became the first caliph and Muslim leader after Muhammad, brought them back under Muslim control and then continued to spread Muslim rule to areas outside of the Arabian Peninsula. The Middle East at that time was controlled by empires that were fighting with one another. The Byzantine Empire controlled the regions of Syria, Egypt, and Turkey. The Sasanian Empire ruled what is now known as Iraq and Iran. Both were weakened by decades of war with each other. They were not prepared for Abu Bakr and his Muslim soldiers coming out of Arabia.

Abu Bakr died shortly after his forces attacked the two empires based in Syria and Iraq. Umar ibn al-Khattab, a strong-willed and effective leader, then took over as the second caliph. During the next ten years under his rule, Muslim armies saw victory after victory. With every win, the borders of the new Muslim empire spread in the Middle East, and the teachings of Islam began to be carried beyond Arabia as Muslims settled in new areas. Umar captured Damascus, Jerusalem, and Egypt in the 630s. By the time Umar died in 644 CE, Muslim armies controlled all of Iraq and much of Iran. Under the next leader, Uthman ibn Affan, the Muslim armies continued to march farther across the hemisphere. They conquered North Africa and the rest of Iran. This territorial expansion continued until Uthman was murdered by his enemies in 656 CE.

The Umayyad and Abbasid Dynasties

Uthman's death led to a dispute among Muslims over who should become the next leader. Ali's proclamation as the fourth caliph and Mu'awiya's opposition to him created an internal struggle that interrupted the Muslim territorial expansion. The Muslim community continued to grow, with some Muslims sympathizing with the views of the Shia, while others, later known as Sunnis, opted to accept any ruler who would restore order and security. Many Muslims chose to follow Uthman's family, the Umayyads, who had gained control as political leaders.

At this point, Muslims were no longer a small community of people who lived near Muhammad in Medina. They now oversaw a large empire, comprising a vast part of the Middle East and North Africa. The Umayyad armies extended Muslim rule, which facilitated Islam's reach westward across Africa over the next one hundred years. They turned northward as well, crossing the Straits of Gibraltar into Spain. They traveled as far as southern France, before reaching the limits of expansion far from the capital at Damascus, signaled by their defeat in 732 CE at the hands of the Frankish king Charles Martel. Other Umayyad armies also drove eastward during that time, conquering lands comprising the modern-day countries of Afghanistan and Pakistan.

The Umayyads, who adopted the doctrines of Sunni Islam being formulated by religious scholars, had many enemies, including the Shiite Muslims. Attacks from these groups weakened the power of the Umayyads. Furthermore, the Umayyad's Arab-centric policies tended to upset Persians and others who had converted to Islam. By 750 CE, the Abbasid family, with origins in Mecca like the Umayyads but with a more open-minded policy toward converts and Shiites, defeated the Umayyads in several battles and gained control of the empire. Their first leader, Abu al-Abbas, ordered that all remaining members of the Umayyad family be killed. The Abbasid dynasty ruled for hundreds of years. Their rule marked a time when Muslim civilization flourished, and many inhabitants of the Muslim empire steadily converted to Islam to join the new "mainstream" culture. The Abbasid empire reached from Egypt to India. The rulers controlled all of the important trade routes in that area and produced large amounts of agricultural products and gained great wealth.

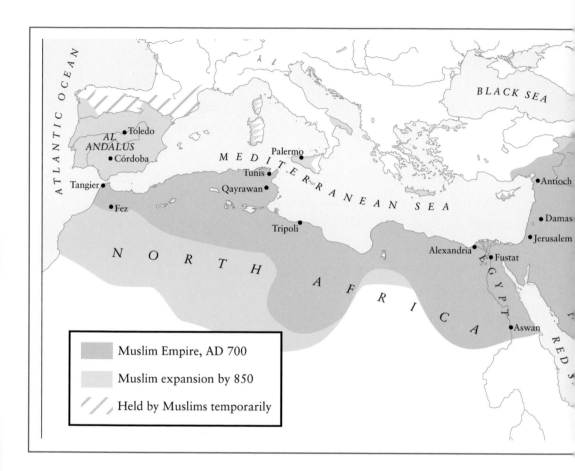

The center of this powerful Muslim world at the time
was Baghdad. It grew into a major city as the Abbasid
capital. Beautiful palaces and magnificent homes were
constructed there. Muslim scholars translated important
works from other cultures, including Greece and India,
increasing the community's knowledge of mathematics,
medicine, and philosophy. An important new legal system
was established as well, based on the Qur'an and the teachings of Muhammad. Great works of art and literature were
created, and Baghdad was made the setting for many of
the tales in *One Thousand and One Nights* (also known

This map shows the spread of the Muslim Empire after Muhammad's death. After Muhammad's close companions served as the first four caliphs, a Muslim dynasty known as the Umayyads oversaw the expansion of Muslim rule. In 750 CE, they were overthrown by another dynasty known as the Abbasids, who ushered in a Golden Age for Islamic society.

as *Arabian Nights*), which is still read today. It was a golden age in which Islam and the Arabic language spread throughout the Middle East, North Africa, Spain, and Central Asia.

However, the Muslim world also began fracturing as it grew. Ambitious provincial governors sought to create their own local dynasties, supported by their own armies and bureaucracies, rather than send taxes to the central government in far-away Baghdad. It became difficult for the central government to directly control all the provinces. In the early thirteenth century, Mongol armies swept across

Abu Zayd, a fictional character, greets some merchants. He is the creation of the eleventh-century poet, scholar, and government official al-Hariri of Basra. The author was also a silk merchant, and it is merchant caravans like the one pictured here that fostered the spread of Islam and the development of a Golden Age of ideas, information, art, and technology.

the lands of modern-day China and Russia and into Central Asia. They eventually made it to Baghdad, which they captured. The city was destroyed in 1258, and the Abbasid leader was killed. This brought an end to one of the most glorious periods in Islamic history. However, Muslim societies continued to thrive in various lands and reach new peaks of cultural achievement.

Three Separate Islamic Empires

The spiritual and cultural beliefs of Muslims were too strong to be extinguished by wars. By the fifteenth century, the Muslim world had once again become powerful. Three separate large empires stretched across an area that went from modern-day Bangladesh to what is now known as Algeria. These new empires had built great societies. The Mughal Empire ruled over the Indian subcontinent, constructing what is still considered one of the most famous buildings in the world, the Taj Mahal. The Safavid dynasty ruled Iran. The Ottoman Empire was established in what is now Turkey, after taking over the capital of the Byzantine Empire and changing its name from Constantinople to Istanbul.

All three empires flourished for centuries, and Muslims of different backgrounds traveled freely through them for trade, pilgrimage, scholarship, and other reasons. Artistic works such as calligraphy and miniature painting were created. Beautiful mosques were erected, as were schools and cultural centers, some of which are still standing today. Commercial activity increased during this period. Merchants bought and sold spices, clothes, and jewels. Ships and camel caravans brought these goods throughout the Middle East and parts of Asia. The traveling merchants and Sufi preachers brought their religion with them into bordering regions. More communities were introduced to the Muslim faith in places such as Indonesia and Central Africa. Once again, Islam spread to new regions as more and more people were converted.

The Power Balance Shifts

Eventually, all of the Islamic empires were weakened by infighting and the rise of European powers. By the nineteenth century, the Safavid and Mughul states had disappeared. The Ottoman Empire came to an end in the early twentieth century. With the emergence of nation states and secularized societies following European colonization of traditionally Muslim territories, Islam would no longer have the same political power or dominance over such a large part of the world as it did in the past. Military, economic, and cultural power gradually shifted to Europe, the United States, and Russia/the Soviet Union. Still, the great Muslim societies that flourished after Muhammad's death spread the religion to all corners of the globe, making Islam one of the world's great religious traditions.

Today, there are 1.2 billion Muslims in the world. People of many races and in many countries have interpreted Islam and developed Islam's rich religious traditions rooted in local cultures and customs. The vast majority of the faithful are peace-loving and fully involved in the evolving global community of nations. Muslims have become an important part of the religious diversity in many countries. Eight million Muslims live in the United States alone.

Islam Today

From the year 610 CE to the present day, Islam has grown tremendously. It now stretches out like a tree, with its roots on the Arabian Peninsula, its trunk in the Middle East, and its branches stretching into many countries as far west as the United States and Canada and as far east as Indonesia and Australia. Its leaves are the many great cross-cultural events and people who practice Islam. In stretching around the world, these branches represent modern Islam and how it is practiced in different countries while remaining loyal to Islamic teachings and values.

Evolving social, economic, and political factors in different Muslim nations have sometimes led to conflict between old and new customs. Western nations have had to grapple with accommodating the religious beliefs and practices of Muslims and other immigrants in the context of their own histories and long-standing cultures. While the conflicts tend to make the front pages of newspapers more often than the peaceful and routine practices of Islam around the world, the global flowering of the Islamic faith has led to some of

A young Muslim woman protests French law prohibiting the wearing of the hijab (head scarf) by scrawling a sign on her head scarf that reads, "Don't touch," in French.

the most fascinating aspects of our rapidly evolving world culture.

The Battle Over Head Scarves

Since the nineteenth century, France has had large numbers of immigrants from Muslim countries in North Africa. According to the British Broadcasting Company (BBC), in 2005, Islam was the second-largest religion in traditionally Catholic Christian France, with approximately five million Muslims from the African countries of Algeria, Morocco, and Tunisia living in suburbs of Paris, Lille, Lyon, Marseilles, and other French cities. Many of these working-class immigrants live in poor neighborhoods, where they tend to isolate themselves. They also face racial and cultural prejudices from mainstream society. France also has its particular approach to religious freedom and civic identity.

In 2004, France banned the wearing of head scarves and religious ornaments in its state schools. Government officials explained the ban as a reflection of French tradition—its strong commitment to a sharp separation of church and state (or religion and the government). Since the French Revolution of the late eighteenth century, it has been an essential part of French culture that one's religious views remain private and are not part of government decision-making or laws; they are strictly kept apart. Therefore, most French citizens agreed with the government's 2004 decision. Yet, it was viewed very differently by many newly arrived Muslim immigrants, who saw it as discriminatory and suppressive.

This ruling challenged some Muslim women's deeply held convictions about what it means to be a good Muslim.

In Islamic culture, women wear the hijab, or head scarf, as a sign of modesty. Many Muslim women in France felt they were being asked to give up their dignity, as well as hide their important religious beliefs. Other Muslims felt that they were being singled out by the French government because their display of religion was more obvious than those of other religious groups. Under the ban, Christians could still wear small crosses to signify their faith, while Muslims had to give up their religious symbols entirely. There were protests by many Muslims all over France, but the government upheld the ruling. As a result, French Muslims practice their religious beliefs without head coverings if they wish to attend state schools.

The Cartoon Controversy

Another example of tension between religious and civic values in increasingly pluralistic societies occurred in Denmark in 2005. Denmark has a long tradition of freedom of the press. When a Danish newspaper published several cartoons about Islam, including one by cartoonist Kurt Westergaard that showed the prophet Muhammad wearing a turban that looked like a bomb, many members of the Muslim community in Denmark and around the world grew very angry and protested against the publication of the image. The cartoonist explained that his cartoon was meant to make the point that some people hide behind Muhammad to explain away their acts of terrorism, but many in the Muslim world didn't interpret his message in that way. Some Muslims believe that it is disrespectful and sacrilegious to show any image of the prophet Muhammad,

Iman: The Five Pillars of Islam

- **Shahadah** The declaration of faith, an affirmation that there is only one true God and that Muhammad is his servant and messenger.
- **Salat** Five prayers throughout each day that consist of reciting prayers from the Qur'an, bowing, and prostrating in worship before God.
- **Sawm** Fasting from sunrise to sunset during Ramadan, the ninth month of the Islamic calendar, to cultivate self-restraint and appreciation for God's bounty.
- **Zakah** Almsgiving; every financially able Muslim is obligated to donate 2.5 percent of his or her wealth to support the needy once every year. Muslims may also offer additional charitable donations throughout the year.
- **Hajj** The pilgrimage to Mecca that each Muslim is expected to make at least once in his or her life, as a commemoration of the patriarch Abraham and a return to the roots of the faith.

while other Muslims were offended by this image of the prophet as a terrorist.

Large protests took place in other European countries in 2006 when more newspapers reprinted the cartoons in order to stand by the Danish newspaper's decision to exercise its

This February 2006 photo, which was taken at the Danish Consulate in New York City, shows a Muslim woman holding a Qur'an and protesting a Danish newspaper's series of cartoons considered to be insulting depictions of the prophet Muhammad.

freedom of the press. Then, even more protests took place in February 2008, when Danish newspapers reprinted the cartoons once again after Danish police arrested several people who were said to be planning to kill the cartoonist Westergaard. In three Afghan cities, youths burned the flags of Western nations and made anti-American and anti-European statements. This incident has raised important questions about the meaning of freedom of expression and its social repercussions. It will take many careful, thoughtful conversations about the interplay of freedom of the press, freedom of speech, religious and cultural norms, and civic values in every pluralistic society among people of various backgrounds and experiences to find ways to coexist with one another.

Love, Muslim Law, and a Traditionally Western Holiday

Valentine's Day is a popular holiday in the Unites States and Canada. It is meant as a day to share one's feelings with friends and romantic partners, and offer tokens of chocolates, candy hearts, flowers, and cards. Given its Western origins, it has not been observed in most Muslim countries in the Middle East, Asia, or Africa. Muslim immigrants to the United States and Europe have learned of it in recent decades, along with other cultural and national holidays of various countries. In the era of globalization, the idea of Valentine's Day has spread and many people in other countries observe it, including some Muslims.

In looking at this one holiday, we can see how attitudes have changed across the Muslim world. While many religious leaders may pronounce the observance of Valentine's Day to be haram, or forbidden by Islamic law (since it tends to encourage dating and the Western norm of romantic/intimate relationships between unmarried individuals), it is seen by some Muslims as an innocent way to celebrate affection for their spouses. Conservative Muslims believe that only a handful of Islamic holidays should be honored and that cultural celebrations such as Valentine's Day conflict with religious teachings and can corrupt Muslim youth. Saudi Arabia bans any celebration of the holiday for these reasons, and it is frowned upon in other countries. However, in

In central Baghdad, a Muslim woman looks at decorations on the eve of the holiday Eid al-Hub, or Feast of Love, akin to the West's St. Valentine's Day.

places as different from each other as the Gaza Strip and Dubai, some Muslims buy treats for loved ones on this day, which is given the Arabic name Eid al-Hub, or Feast of Love. According to an article by the Associated Press in February 2008, flower shops in Bahrain imported around 150,000 roses in one week, and small boats on the Nile River in Cairo, Egypt, were decorated with red ribbons and flashing red hearts.

One flower shop in Gaza was even selling roses it had smuggled in from Israel, hidden under the sheets of medical patients. The shopkeeper of Rose Flower Shop snuck them in with Gazan residents being treated in Israeli hospitals who returned home before the fourteenth. He managed to get five hundred roses this way.

International travel, trade, satellite television, and especially the Internet have brought Muslims in contact with the wider world, whether in Pakistan, Paris, or the Palestinian territories. The observance of Valentine's Day indicates that the world is more connected than ever before. It is also a vivid illustration of how aspects of Western culture are challenged and adopted in various Muslim societies.

It's no surprise that a religion as beautiful, rich, and meaningful as Islam continues to shape today's world. It is often a force for uniting individuals and families in the pursuit of the values of kindness, compassion, and responsibility to others that Muhammad exemplified more than 1,300 years ago. Its vivid history is not forgotten as it grows in different societies shaped by modernity. And its story continues today, even if cultural changes and new religious interpretations come as a result of Islam being practiced in many different areas of the globe. Muslims of today seek new ways to preserve their beliefs and values in a world that is growing both bigger (farther away from its Middle Eastern origins) and smaller (drawn closer together through global integration and communication). As the tree of Islam grows, it will no doubt continue to enrich the lives, hearts, and souls of those who shelter in its shade.

GLOSSARY

Allah The Arabic word for the One God.

Eid al-Fitr The feast day that Muslims celebrate to signal the end of Ramadan.

hadith Accounts of what Muhammad said and did during his lifetime; usually these involve stories of his acts of kindness and wisdom.

imam The leader of the Salat prayer service at a mosque; also a term for the early leaders of Islam and highly regarded religious scholars in Islamic society.

monotheism The belief that there is only one God.

Qur'an The scripture of Islam that contains all of the revelations that the angel Gabriel dictated to Muhammad as guidance from God.

Ramadan The month of fasting and prayer that Muslim faithful undertake once a year to cultivate self-restraint and humility before God, as one of the pillars of Islam.

sectarian Actions and beliefs motivated by fierce allegiance to a particular sect, or religious group.

sharia The way, or law, of Islam that is produced by scholars by interpreting the Qur'an and sunnah (Muhammad's teachings and life example).

Shiite Muslim Historically, members of the party of Ali; Muslims who believe that Ali, then Ali's son Hussein and other descendents, were the rightful caliphs (successors) as part of Muhammad's bloodline.

Sunni Muslim Muslims who respect the first four caliphs as "rightly guided" leaders who faithfully followed Muhammad's sunnah, or life's customs. Sunnis accepted subsequent political rulers of various types.

Ta'ziyah The Shiite passion play the reenacts the events surrounding Hussein's death at Karbala in 680 and commemorates him as a selfless martyr.

Ulama Religious scholars throughout Islamic history who have interpreted the Qur'an and sunnah to explain theological concepts, develop Islamic law, and provide guidance to Muslims on questions of belief and practice.

FOR MORE INFORMATION

The Islamic Center of America
19500 Ford Road
Dearborn, MI 48128
(313) 593-0000
Web site: http://www.icofa.com/index.html
The Islamic Center of America is dedicated to the education of the general public and the spiritual growth and betterment of its community. The Islamic Center has a rich history of education and community leadership, sharing its faith and house of worship with all those who are interested in learning about Islam and Muslims.

Islamic Society of North America (ISNA)
P.O. Box 38
Plainfield, IN 46168
(317) 839-8157
Web site: http://www.isna.net
This organization seeks to educate North American Muslims and promote cooperation with other faiths and peoples.

Muslim Association of Canada (MAC)
332-1568 Merivale Road
Ottawa, ON K2G 5Y7
Canada
(613) 321-5000

Web site: http://www.macnet.ca
This nonprofit organization provides social services for the Muslim
population of Canada and provides education about Islam to
non-Muslim Canadians.

Muslim Public Affairs Council (MPAC)
110 Maryland Avenue NE, Suite 210
Washington, DC 20002
(202) 547-7701
Web site: http://www.mpac.org
MPAC is a public service agency working for the civil rights of
American Muslims, for the integration of Islam into American
pluralism, and for a positive, constructive relationship between
American Muslims and their representatives.

Muslim Students Association National (MSAN)
MSA of the U.S. and Canada
P.O. Box 1096
Falls Church, VA 22041
(703) 820-7900
Web site: http://www.msanational.org
The MSAN promotes and helps link Muslim student associations
on college and university campuses throughout North America.

The Prince Alwaleed Center for
Muslim-Christian Understanding
Georgetown University
ICC 260 3700 O Street NW
Washington, DC 20057

(202) 687-8375
Web site: http://cmcu.georgetown.edu
This Georgetown University center of learning specializes in Muslim
and Muslim-Christian issues and initiatives.

Web Sites

Due to the changing nature of Internet links, Rosen
Publishing has developed an online list of Web sites related
to the subject of this book. This site is updated regularly.
Please use this link to access this list:

http://www.rosenlinks.com/ui/hoi

FOR FURTHER READING

Baines, Fran, ed. *Islam* (Eyewitness Books). New York, NY: DK Publishing, 2005.

Barnes, Trevor. *Islam* (World Faiths). New York, NY: Kingfisher, 2005.

Demi. *Muhammad*. New York, NY: Margaret K. McElderry, 2003.

Douglass, Susan L. *Ramadan* (On My Own Holidays). Minneapolis, MN: Carolrhoda Books, 2003.

Ganeri, Anita. *This Is My Faith: Islam*. Hauppauge, NY: Barron's Educational Series, 2006.

Gordon, Matthew S. *Islam* (World Religions). New York, NY: Facts on File, Inc., 2006.

Khan, Rukhsana. *Muslim Child: Understanding Islam Through Stories and Poems*. Morton Grove, IL: Albert Whitman & Company, 2002.

Thompson, Joy. *Islam* (World Faiths). London, England: Chrysalis Children's Books, 2005.

Wormser, Richard. *American Islam: Growing Up Muslim in America*. New York, NY: Walker Books for Young Readers, 2002.

Young, Mitchell, ed. *Religions and Religious Movements: Islam*. Farmington Hills, MI: Greenhaven Press, 2005.

BIBLIOGRAPHY

Armstrong, Karen. *Islam: A Short History*. New York, NY: Modern Library, 2002.

BBC. "Headscarf Defeat Riles French Muslims." November 1, 2005. Retrieved March 2008 (http://news.bbc.co.uk/2/hi/europe/4395934.stm).

Cleary, Thomas, ed. *The Essential Qur'an: The Heart of Islam*. New York, NY: HarperCollins Publishers, 1994.

Denny, Frederick M. *Islam* (Religious Traditions of the World). San Francisco, CA: Harper San Francisco, 1987.

Denny, Frederick M. *Islam and the Muslim Community*. Long Grove, IL: Waveland Press, Inc., 1987.

Gordon, Matthew S. *Islam: Origins, Practices, Holy Texts, Sacred Persons, Sacred Places*. Oxford, England: Oxford University Press, 2002.

Grieve, Paul. *A Brief Guide to Islam: History, Faith, and Politics: The Complete Introduction*. New York, NY: Carroll and Graf Publishers, 2006.

Hamidullah, Muhammad. "Biography of Muhammad." *Introduction to Islam*. Centre Culturel Islamique, 1969. Retrieved January 2008 (http://muhammad.net/bio/profbio.html).

Laub, Karin. "Gaza Notes Forbidden Valentine's Day." *USA Today*, February 14, 2008. Retrieved February 15, 2008 (http://www.usatoday.com/news/world/2008-02-14-3717676999_x.htm).

Miller, John, and Aaron Kenedi, eds. *Inside Islam: The Faith, the People, and the Conflicts of the World's Fastest-Growing Religion.* New York, NY: Marlowe & Company, 2002.

Nasir, Octavia, and Pam Benson. "Purported bin Laden Message Condemns Europe." CNN, March 19, 2008. Retrieved March 2008 (http://www.cnn.com/2008/ WORLD/meast/03/19/binladen.message/index. html?iref=mpstoryview).

Sardar, Ziauddin. *Desperately Seeking Paradise: Journeys of a Skeptical Muslim.* London, England: Granta Books, 2004.

Sultan, Sahib. *The Qur'an for Dummies.* Hoboken, NJ: Wiley Publishing, Inc., 2004.

Waines, David. *An Introduction to Islam.* Cambridge, England: Cambridge University Press, 2003.

INDEX

About the Author

Frances O'Connor is a former New York City high school teacher and the author of several books for teenagers. She started her publishing career in the religion division of a major book publisher.

About the Consultant

Munir Shaikh oversees research and consulting activities at the Institute on Religion and Civic Values (IRCV), a non-advocacy organization with expertise in world religions, world history, civil society, pluralism, and related subjects. Munir has a master's degree in Islamic Studies from the University of California, Los Angeles, and has over fifteen years of experience in writing and editing texts pertaining to Islamic history and culture.

Photo Credits